"The entrance of

Introduction to Typology and Symbolism

An Expository Study of Types and Symbols Found in the Bible

"The entrance of your words gives light."
–Psalm 119:130

Introduction to Typology and Symbolism

An Expository Study of Types and Symbols Found in the Bible

Dr. S. Walker

Introduction to Typology and Symbolism

ISBN 0-9724220-2-1

Published by:
Sheila Walker
S. Walker Publications
P. O. Box 164048
Orlando, FL 32716
www.swalkerpublications.com

Printed in the United States of America

Scripture quotations taken from the *King James Version of The Holy Bible*

Cover Photo: Dr. S. Walker

Volume 1: Introduction to Bible Doctrine
A Systematic Study of Seven Doctrines of the Christian Faith—Made Easy
Volume 2: Introduction to Bible Origin
A Study of the Formation of the Bible
Volume 3: Introduction to Typology and Symbolism
An Expository Study of Types and Symbols Found in the Bible

CONTENTS

Introduction to Typology and Symbolism explains the meanings of divine figures of speech found in the Scriptures. The typical and symbolic meaning of names, places, articles, animals, colors and other ways that God expressed Himself, are brought to light in this volume. From Genesis to Revelation, types and symbols bring the Old and New Testaments in harmony with the theme of God's Word . . . salvation through Jesus Christ.

Using an expository method, ***Introduction to Typology and Symbolism*** focuses on the most frequent types and symbols found in the Bible so that they can be easily understood. This volume promises to enrich your insight and give you a deeper understanding of the Scriptures.

"The entrance of your words gives light."
Psalm 119:130

Introduction to Types and Symbols

The Bible speaks mainly of God's love, plan and purpose for His creation. In the early stages, the relationship between God and man became marred by man's sin and disobedience. Although he had assistance from his adversary, man's own human nature was to blame for the failed relationship with God. Unable to reconcile and repair the breach, God employed His own plan of redemption through Jesus Christ. This brings to light the entire theme of the Bible. From Genesis through Revelation, the plan of God's salvation is unfolded. God used typical language to illustrate the things that were to come in execution of His divine purpose.

A type is a divine illustration of something that is forthcoming. These divine illustrations may be in the form of a person, an event, a thing, ceremonies or an institution. Because of the nature of types, they are also considered to be prophetic. Furthermore, a type must have an antitype (that which it speaks of) or its fulfillment.

Types play an important role in Scripture because they link the Old Testament with the New Testament, which reveals the consistency of God's plan of redemption. The discovery of types brings hope to the heart of the reader of God's Word. Old Testament types relate to man's need for deliverance and salvation. The antitypes found in the New Testament reveal the fulfillment of that need provided by God through Jesus Christ . . . man's redeemer.

Guidelines to Interpreting Types

1. Types reveal the intention of God using prophetic language.
2. Types (unlike Bible prophecy) do not need prophetic interpretation.
3. Due to its prophetic nature, types must have an antitype or fulfillment (found mostly in the New Testament).
4. Types that do not have a New Testament fulfillment should be recognized as symbolic illustrations, which are to be used as analogies only.
5. When making an interpretation, consider resemblance, characteristics, and usage of scriptural content before concluding the discovery of a type.
6. Remember that types connect Scriptures and demonstrate the consistency of God's Word. Therefore, one's personal interpretation of a type or symbol cannot be viewed as a divine truth. God has already declared His truth through the Word for our learning.

2 Timothy 3:16 "All scripture is given by inspiration of God, and is profitable for doctrine, for reproof, for correction, for instruction in righteousness."

7. Types and symbols are different. A symbol is something that represents something else and is usually a material object. Symbols, unlike types, can be found in both testaments. ❖

CHAPTER 1

LESSONS IN TYPES

Aim: To explore the illustrations of types (through people, events, things, institutions and ceremonies) as a demonstration for further discovery and usage.

LESSON ONE — A TYPE OF PERSON

Romans 5:14 "Nevertheless death reigned from Adam to Moses, even over them that had not sinned after the similitude of Adam's transgression, who is the figure of him that was to come."

Question: Who is "Him" in the Scripture?
Answer: Jesus Christ.

Comparing Adam with Jesus through research of the Scriptures we learn that:

Both are referred to as Adam.

The first Adam was created and became a living soul.
The second Adam (Jesus Christ) became a life giving Spirit.

The first man (Adam) was formed from the earth.
The second man (illustrated by Jesus) is from heaven.

From one man's transgression (Adam) many died. (Romans 5:15)
From one man (Jesus Christ) the grace of God abounded to many. (Romans 5:17)

Through one man's disobedience (Adam) many were made sinners.
Through one man's obedience (Jesus) many were made righteous.

Through one man sin reigned in death (Adam).
Through one man (Jesus) grace can reign through righteousness to eternal life.

LESSON TWO—TYPE OF EVENT

1st Corinthians 10:11 "Now all these things happened unto them for ensamples: and they are written for our admonition, upon whom the ends of the world are come."

Question: What event is being referred to in this Scripture?

Answer: The wilderness experience of Israel.

Research the story of Israel's trip through the wilderness in Exodus 12:31 and Numbers 33:94

Question: What is the nature of this illustration as it relates to being a type?

Answer: This type foreshadows an event that can happen in our lives. It teaches us that we may go through a wilderness experience and that we should remember how God dealt with Israel as guidelines for our own experience.

In this illustration we learn that Israel:

- Had a direction to follow to get through the experience.
- Was guided by God by a pillar of cloud and a pillar of fire.
- Was given spiritual food and water.

Question: How would you apply this to your own life?

Answer: The life of Israel in the wilderness is typical of Christian life. We are sure to experience difficult times or transitions but we should always remember that God is with us and has a direction He wants us to follow. He will guide us and provide for us until we get through it. Knowing this, we should remain faithful and refrain from worldly desires which may easily be obtained.

LESSON THREE—A TYPE OF THING

Hebrews 10:20 "By a new and living way, which he hath consecrated for us, through the veil, that is to say, his flesh."

Question: What is the "thing" this Scripture is referring to?

Answer: The veil that hung in the temple to keep the place where God dwelt separated.

Question: What is the "veil" a type of?

Answer: It is a type of Christ's flesh. When He died, the veil (which prevented access directly to God because of sin), was torn down. Being redeemed once and for all by Christ, we now have access directly to God.

No longer is there a partition, we can now go boldly to the throne of grace.

Research Scriptures that support this truth. For example John 14:6

Lesson Four—A Type of Institution

Hebrews 9:11 "But Christ being come an high priest of good things to come, by a greater and more perfect tabernacle, not made with hands, that is to say, not of this building."

Question: What is the type in this Scripture?
Answer: The Tabernacle, which was a Holy place where the regulations of the first covenant (The Law), was carried out.

Question: What were some of the regulations or functions that were carried out in the Tabernacle?
Answer: Cleansing, Confession, Sacrifices, Offerings, Prayers and Intercession (which were done by the Priests and the High Priest).

Research the Tabernacle in Leviticus and cross-reference with Hebrews Chapter 9.

Question: Why is the Tabernacle a type of the Perfect Tabernacle (which is not a copy of the one made with hands)?
Answer: Because the Perfect Tabernacle is heavenly with a High Priest who has made atonement once and for all. This heavenly Tabernacle is "perfect" because our High Priest took the "perfect" offering directly to God.

Question: Who is the High Priest and what was his "perfect" sacrifice?
Answer: Christ is the High Priest who made Himself the "perfect" sacrifice.

Lesson Five—A Type of Ceremony

1st Corinthians 5:7 "Purge out therefore the old leaven, that ye may be a new lump, as ye are unleavened. For even Christ our Passover is sacrificed for us."

A ceremony is an occasion that requires formal and appropriate behavior. It may also involve participation in rituals that are associated with the occasion. In this Scripture, the occasion is the Passover which was one of the most important festivals for the Jews and was celebrated with great respect in commemoration of their deliverance from bondage. The Passover meal included bitter herbs, unleavened bread and the Pascal Lamb, all of which were symbolic of the Exodus, which was told as part of the ceremony.

Research the events of the night before the Jews left Egypt found in the Book of Exodus.

THE PASCAL LAMB SUMMARIZED:

- The lamb was roasted whole without any of its bones broken.
- On the night it was slain, it was to be eaten entirely with bitter herbs and the carcass was to be burned.
- The blood of the lamb was to be sprinkled on the upper and side door-posts.

Question: How does the summary of the Pascal Lamb relate to Christ and Salvation?

Answer: Without having any of His bones broken, Christ was slain for our sins. When salvation is presented to us, we must accept it in its entirety. This resembles the carcass of the lamb being burned. When judgement came from God upon Egypt, it passed the houses where the blood was applied to the doorposts. After receiving salvation through Jesus Christ, we are not judged with the world and have redemptive rights. Worldly judgement passes over us because of the blood of Christ.

Question: What is leaven?

Answer: Leaven is a fermenting yeast used as a rising ingredient in bread.

Question: What does it typify?

Answer: It typifies sin. In this Scripture, those who are in Christ can have the urge to sin purged from their hearts, making it difficult to rise again and cause sinful acts. We are reminded of this as Christ died for us providing deliverance from the tendency to commit willful sin.

Understanding the typology of the Passover, we should celebrate our deliverance from the bondage of sin often with reverence and great appreciation for what God has provided for us through Jesus Christ, our Lord. ❖

NOTES

NOTES

CHAPTER 2

TYPES AND SYMBOLS

Aaron—A type of Christ; our High Priest who is called of God to offer sacrifices for our sins. The office of the High Priest, although honorable, was held with humility. The High Priest (who was taken out of the general population) was acquainted with the infirmities of the people he represented.

Exodus 28:1 "And take thou unto thee Aaron thy brother, and his sons with him, from among the children of Israel, that he may minister unto me in the priest's office, even Aaron, Nadab and Abihu, Eleazar and Ithamar, Aaron's sons."

Hebrews 5:1-4 "For every high priest taken from among men is ordained for men in things pertaining to God, that he may offer both gifts and sacrifices for sins: Who can have compassion on the ignorant, and on them that are out of the way; for that he himself also is compassed with infirmity. And by reason hereof he ought, as for the people, so also for himself, to offer for sins. And no man taketh this honour unto himself, but he that is called of God, as was Aaron."

Aaron's Rod—The word rod in Scripture typifies power. Serpents are symbolic of Satan or evil. "Aaron's Rod" represents the power of life (good) that has victory over death (evil).

Exodus 7:12 "For they cast down every man his rod, and they became serpents: but Aaron's rod swallowed up their rods."

1st Corinthians 15:54-57 "So when this corruptible shall have put on incorruption, and this mortal shall have put on immortality, then shall be brought to pass the saying that is written, Death is swallowed up in victory. O death, where is thy sting? O grave, where is thy victory? The sting of death is sin; and the strength of sin is the law. But thanks be to God, which giveth us the victory through our Lord Jesus Christ."

Abel—A type of spiritual man who recognized his sins and gave the sacrifice required by God for atonement (meaning to cover). *(Read Hebrews 11:4)*

Genesis 4:4 "And Abel, he also brought of the firstlings of his flock and of the fat thereof. And the LORD had respect unto Abel and to his offering."

Hebrews 9:22 "And almost all things are by the law purged with blood; and without shedding of blood is no remission."

Abraham—A type of God our Father who, without reservation, was willing to sacrifice his only son.

Genesis 22:9 "And they came to the place which God had told him of; and Abraham built an altar there, and laid the wood in order, and bound Isaac his son, and laid him on the altar upon the wood."

John 3:16 "For God so loved the world, that he gave his only begotten Son, that whosoever believeth in him should not perish, but have everlasting life."

Acacia Wood—(Shittim Wood) was used to build the Tabernacle and some of its furniture, it symbolizes the humility of Christ.

Exodus 26:15 "And thou shalt make boards for the tabernacle of shittim wood standing up."

Adam—A contrast to Christ. Adam as a "son of God" was the first natural man and headed the natural race. Christ is "the Son of God," the first of the spiritual sons of God, and is the head of the spiritual race. Through Adam, sin and death is experienced. Yet, through Christ, grace and life is gained. Adam headed the fall of the human race. But through Christ, man is given life. Adam was a living soul, while Christ, is a life-giving Spirit.

Genesis 5:1 "This is the book of the generations of Adam. In the day that God created man, in the likeness of God made he him."

John 3:6 "That which is born of the flesh is flesh; and that which is born of the Spirit is spirit."

1st Corinthians 15:22 "For as in Adam all die, even so in Christ shall all be made alive."

Genesis 2:7 "And the LORD God formed man of the dust of the ground, and breathed into his nostrils the breath of life; and man became a living soul."

John 1:4 "In him was life; and the life was the light of men."

Amalek—The Amalekites waged consistent battle with Israel. Amalek, their "forefather" is a type of "flesh" that is in conflict within the believer.

Exodus 17:8 "Then came Amalek, and fought with Israel in Rephidim."

Galatians 4:29 "But as then he that was born after the flesh persecuted him that was born after the Spirit, even so it is now."

Ark (Noah's)—Christ is a safe-haven in the time of trouble for the believer. The Ark is a type of Christ that typifies salvation. The Ark was protected against the judgement of the flood waters because it had been sealed with pitch. The safe place for believers (which is Christ) is sealed with His blood. Pitch translated means "atonement." *(Read Leviticus 17:11)*

Genesis 6:14—"Make thee an ark of gopher wood; rooms shalt thou make in the ark, and shalt pitch it within and without with pitch."

Hebrews 11:7 "By faith Noah, being warned of God of things not seen as yet, moved with fear, prepared an ark to the saving of his house; by the which he condemned the world, and became heir of the righteousness which is by faith."

Asenath—Asenath was a gentile wife that was given to Joseph during the time he was rejected by his brothers. Similarly, Christ was given the "Church" which is made up of believers who are called out from Gentiles after He was rejected by His brethren. "Church" is translated "ecclessia" meaning "called out assembly."

Genesis 41:45 "And Pharaoh called Joseph's name Zaphnathpaaneah; and he gave him to wife Asenath the daughter of Potipherah priest of On. And Joseph went out over all the land of Egypt."

Acts 15:14 "Simeon hath declared how God at the first did visit the Gentiles, to take out of them a people for his name."

Atonement—Covering for sin was necessary to receive divine forgiveness. The blood of bulls and goats was not meant to take away sin, but rather it was confession of sin to provide temporary appeasement. The offenses of the sinner was then "passed-over," being covered until God provided the "once and for all" sacrifice . . . Jesus Christ. *(Read Hebrews Chapter 10)*

Leviticus 23:27 "Also on the tenth day of this seventh month there shall be a day of atonement: it shall be an holy convocation unto you; and ye shall afflict your souls, and offer an offering made by fire unto the LORD."

Hebrews 10:9-10 "Then said he, Lo, I come to do thy will, O God. He taketh away the first, that he may establish the second. By the which will we are sanctified through the offering of the body of Jesus Christ once for all."

Anointing Oil—Applied to objects and people that are separated unto God, making them sanctified for His use. Anointing oil is a symbol of the Holy Spirit who separates and sanctifies. *(Read Acts 1:8)*

Leviticus 8:10-13 "And Moses took the anointing oil, and anointed the tabernacle and all that *was* therein, and sanctified them. And he sprinkled thereof upon the altar seven times, and anointed the altar and all his vessels, both the laver and his foot, to sanctify them. And he poured of the anointing oil upon Aaron's head, and anointed him, to sanctify him. And Moses brought Aaron's sons, and put coats upon them, and girded them with girdles, and put bonnets upon them; as the LORD commanded Moses."

Babylon—Is the Greek form of the Hebrew word "babel" which means confusion (describing Gentile social order). The city of Babylon is used prophetically by the prophet Isaiah who describes the Gentile political system ("times of the Gentile"). John describes the world's corrupt religious and political systems in the book of Revelation. *(Read Isaiah 13:11-18)*

Isaiah 13:19-22 "And Babylon, the glory of kingdoms, the beauty of the Chaldees' excellency, shall be as when God overthrew Sodom and Gomorrah. It shall never be inhabited, neither shall it be dwelt in from generation to generation: neither shall the Arabian pitch tent there; neither shall the shepherds make their fold there. But wild beasts of the desert shall lie there; and their houses shall be full of doleful creatures; and owls shall dwell there, and satyrs shall dance there. And the wild beasts of the islands shall cry in their desolate houses, and dragons in their pleasant palaces: and her time is near to come, and her days shall not be prolonged."

Revelation 18:2 "And he cried mightily with a strong voice, saying, Babylon the great is fallen, is fallen, and is become the habitation of devils, and the hold of every foul spirit, and a cage of every unclean and hateful bird."

Balaam (the way of Balaam)—Symbolizes the intent to lure the people of God into error.

2nd Peter 2:15—"Which have forsaken the right way, and are gone astray, following the way of Balaam the son of Bosor, who loved the wages of unrighteousness."

Beast—A symbol of world kingdoms, empires, cruel and cunning leaders, ungodliness. "Times of the Gentiles" as seen in apocalyptic Scriptures. *(Read Luke 21:24, Revelation 16:19)*

Daniel 7:8 "I considered the horns, and, behold, there came up among them another little horn, before whom there were three of the first horns plucked up by the roots: and, behold, in this horn were eyes like the eyes of man, and a mouth speaking great things."

Benjamin—The name Rachel gave her son before dying from childbirth means, "son of sorrow." Seeing him differently, Jacob called him Benjamin (meaning "son of my right hand") who grew to head the victorious tribe that allied itself with Judah. Benjamin therefore is a double type of Christ. Although Christ brought sorrow to His mother, He brought salvation and victory to believers.

Genesis 35:18 "And it came to pass, as her soul was in departing, (for she died) that she called his name Ben-oni: but his father called him Benjamin."

Luke 2:32-35 "A light to lighten the Gentiles, and the glory of thy people Israel. And Joseph and his mother marvelled at those things which were spoken of him. And Simeon blessed them, and said unto Mary his mother,

Behold, this child is set for the fall and rising again of many in Israel; and for a sign which shall be spoken against; (Yea, a sword shall pierce through thy own soul also,) that the thoughts of many hearts may be revealed."

Black—A color that is symbolic of death, mourning and famine.

Jeremiah 14:1-3 "The word of the LORD that came to Jeremiah concerning the dearth. Judah mourneth, and the gates thereof languish; they are black unto the ground; and the cry of Jerusalem is gone up. And their nobles have sent their little ones to the waters: they came to the pits, and found no water; they returned with their vessels empty; they were ashamed and confounded, and covered their heads."

Brazen Altar—A type of cross where Christ offered Himself as a sacrifice for our sins. *(Read Hebrews 10:5-14)*

Exodus 27:1 "And thou shalt make an altar of shittim wood, five cubits long, and five cubits broad; the altar shall be foursquare: and the height thereof shall be three cubits."

Hebrews 9:14 "How much more shall the blood of Christ, who through the eternal Spirit offered himself without spot to God, purge your conscience from dead works to serve the living God?"

Cain—The characteristics of an earthly man whose practice of religion is void of the need of atonement for sin. He is self-willed, unregenerate and more natural than spiritual, a contrast to the character of his brother Abel. *(Read Numbers 16 and Hebrews 11:4)*

Genesis 4:3 "And in the process of time it came to pass, that Cain brought of the fruit of the ground an offering unto the LORD."

Jude 11 "Woe unto them! for they have gone in the way of Cain, and ran greedily after the error of Balaam for reward, and perished in the gainsaying of Core."

Candlestick, Golden—Natural light was not allowed in the Tabernacle. Light was obtained from the glow of candlesticks. This light typifies Christ who is our spiritual light that shines in darkness. It also speaks of the believers spirituality and ability to be light bearers. *(Read Matthew 5:14-16)*

Exodus 26:35- "And thou shalt set the table without the veil, and the candlestick over against the table on the side of the tabernacle toward the south: and thou shalt put the table on the north side."

John 8:12 "Then spake Jesus again unto them, saying, I am the light of the world: he that followeth me shall not walk in darkness, but shall have the light of life."

Chariots and Horses—Chariots represent speed and warfare, horses represent strength and conquest. Both are powerful, symbolizing the judgement of God. *(Read Zechariah 10:3)*

Isaiah 66:15 "For, behold, the LORD will come with fire, and with his chariots like a whirlwind, to render his anger with fury, and his rebuke with flames of fire."

Zechariah 6:1 "And I turned, and lifted up mine eyes, and looked, and, behold, there came four chariots out from between two mountains; and the mountains were mountains of brass."

Coats of skins—The innocent is slain to provide a covering for the sinner so that they can be presented before God. This divine provision typifies Christ providing righteousness for us.

Genesis 3:21 "Unto Adam also and to his wife did the LORD God make coats of skins, and clothed them."

Revelation 19:8 "And to her was granted that she should be arrayed in fine linen, clean and white: for the fine linen is the righteousness of saints."

Cup—Symbolic of prosperity and condemnation by God.

Psalm 23:5 "Thou preparest a table before me in the presence of mine enemies: thou anointest my head with oil; my cup runneth over."

Psalm 11:6 "Upon the wicked he shall rain snares, fire and brimstone, and an horrible tempest: this shall be the portion of their cup."

Cup of:

Consolation

Jeremiah 16:7 "Neither shall men tear themselves for them in mourning, to comfort them for the dead; neither shall men give them the cup of consolation to drink for their father or for their mother."

Salvation

Psalm 116:13 "I will take the cup of salvation, and call upon the name of the LORD."

Blessing

1st Corinthians 10:16 "The cup of blessing which we bless, is it not the communion of the blood of Christ? The bread which we break, is it not the communion of the body of Christ?"

The Lord

1st Corinthians 10:21 "Ye cannot drink the cup of the Lord, and the cup of devils: ye cannot be partakers of the Lord's table, and of the table of devils."

Fury

***Isaiah* 51:17-22** "Awake, awake, stand up, O Jerusalem, which hast drunk at the hand of the LORD the cup of his fury; thou hast drunken the dregs of the cup of trembling, and wrung them out. There is none to guide her among all the sons whom she hath brought forth; neither is there any that taketh her by the hand of all the sons that she hath brought up. These two things are come unto thee; who shall be sorry for thee? desolation, and destruction, and the famine, and the sword: by whom shall I comfort thee? Thy sons have fainted, they lie at the head of all the streets, as a wild bull in a net: they are full of the fury of the LORD, the rebuke of thy God. Therefore hear now this, thou afflicted, and drunken, but not with wine: Thus saith thy Lord the LORD, and thy God that pleadeth the cause of his people, Behold, I have taken out of thine hand the cup of trembling, even the dregs of the cup of my fury; thou shalt no more drink it again."

Indignation

Revelation 14:10 "The same shall drink of the wine of the wrath of God, which is poured out without mixture into the cup of his indignation; and he shall be tormented with fire and brimstone in the presence of the holy angels, and in the presence of the Lamb."

David—A type of Christ, who after caring for and protecting his sheep as a good shepherd is given rulership over Israel. *(Read Isaiah 9:6 and Luke 1:32)*

1st Chronicles 17:7 "Now therefore thus shalt thou say unto my servant David, Thus saith the LORD of hosts, I took thee from the sheepcote, even from following the sheep, that thou shouldest be ruler over my people Israel."

Acts 15:16 "After this I will return, and will build again the tabernacle of David, which is fallen down; and I will build again the ruins thereof, and I will set it up."

Egypt—Symbol of the world, world systems or worldliness (cosmos); bondage.

Revelation 11:8 "And their dead bodies shall lie in the street of the great city, which spiritually is called Sodom and Egypt, where also our Lord was crucified."

Ezekiel 23:27 "Thus will I make thy lewdness to cease from thee, and thy whoredom brought from the land of Egypt: so that thou shalt not lift up thine eyes unto them, nor remember Egypt any more."

Enoch—Noah witnessed and survived the judgement of the flood. Enoch, however, did not see God's judgement because he was translated (caught-up). Both are types of people of the apocalyptic judgement. Noah, a type of Jewish people, remain but are kept during the judgement. Enoch, a type of the saints, will not see the judgement because, they will be raptured. *(Read Hebrews 11:7 and Revelation 12:17)*

***Genesis* 5:24** "And Enoch walked with God: and he was not; for God took him."

***Hebrews* 11:5** "By faith Enoch was translated that he should not see death; and was not found, because God had translated him: for before his translation he had this testimony, that he pleased God."

Esau—Despising and not having value for the spirituality of his birthright; Esau is a type of earthly man who disrespects spiritual things.

***Genesis* 25:25** "And the first came out red, all over like an hairy garment; and they called his name Esau."

***Hebrews* 12:15-17** "Looking diligently lest any man fail of the grace of God; lest any root of bitterness springing up trouble you, and thereby many be defiled; Lest there be any fornicator, or profane person, as Esau, who for one morsel of meat sold his birthright. For ye know how that afterward, when he would have inherited the blessing, he was rejected: for he found no place of repentance, though he sought it carefully with tears."

Eve—A type of Church; the bride of Christ which is comprised of the saints who have remained righteous, adorned and kept by the Holy Spirit. The Bride of Christ is in contrast to the adulterous wife of Jehovah—Israel who was later restored. Jehovah's wife sought after another and cannot therefore be characterized as a bride or virgin. The Church on the other hand will remain faithful until the groom comes for her. *(Read Isaiah 54:1-10, Hosea 2:23, 2 Corinthians 11:2 and Revelation 19: 7-8)*

***Genesis* 2:23** "And Adam said, This is now bone of my bones, and flesh of my flesh: she shall be called Woman, because she was taken out of Man."

***John* 3:28-29** "Ye yourselves bear me witness, that I said, I am not the Christ, but that I am sent before him. He that hath the bride is the bridegroom: but the friend of the bridegroom, which standeth and heareth him, rejoiceth greatly because of the bridegroom's voice: this my joy therefore is fulfilled."

Flock—Symbolic of the people of God, gathered together and shepherded by Christ. *(Read Isaiah 40:11)*

***John* 10:16** "And other sheep I have, which are not of this fold: them also I must bring, and they shall hear my voice; and there shall be one fold, and one shepherd."

Fire—Symbolic of the Holiness of God. First, in judgement; second, the manifestation of God; and third, the process of purification. *(Read Mark 9:43-48, Exodus 13:21 and Malachi 3:3)*

Leviticus 1:8-9 "And the priests, Aaron's sons, shall lay the parts, the head, and the fat, in order upon the wood that is on the fire, which is upon the altar. But his inwards and his legs shall he wash in water: and the priest shall burn all on the altar, to be a burnt sacrifice, an offering made by fire, of a sweet savour unto the LORD."

Frankincense—Used as a fragrance, it symbolizes pure worship, prayer, and praise. It is also symbolic of perfection. Unlike incense, frankincense has no formula. Its purity describes the perfection of Christ.

Leviticus 2:1-2 "And when any will offer a meat offering unto the LORD, his offering shall be of fine flour; and he shall pour oil upon it, and put frankincense thereon: And he shall bring it to Aaron's sons the priests: and he shall take thereout his handful of the flour thereof, and of the oil thereof, with all the frankincense thereof; and the priest shall burn the memorial of it upon the altar, to be an offering made by fire, of a sweet savour unto the LORD."

Exodus 30:34 "And the LORD said unto Moses, Take unto thee sweet spices, stacte, and onycha, and galbanum; these sweet spices with pure frankincense: of each shall there be a like weight:"

Garment—A clean and pure garment symbolizes the imputed righteousness of Christ, rather than the believers own self-righteousness, which includes bad morals and ethics. *(Read Philippians 3:6-9)*

Revelation 19:8 "And to her was granted that she should be arrayed in fine linen, clean and white: for the fine linen is the righteousness of saints."

Goat—A type of sinner. In the offerings it typifies Christ, who is a substitute for the sinner. He voluntarily made Himself to be "like" a sinner to die a sinner's death. *(Read Isaiah 53:12; Luke 23:33 and 2nd Corinthians 5:21)*

Leviticus 1:3 "If his offering be a burnt sacrifice of the herd, let him offer a male without blemish: he shall offer it of his own voluntary will at the door of the tabernacle of the congregation before the LORD."

Galatians 3:13 "Christ hath redeemed us from the curse of the law, being made a curse for us: for it is written, Cursed is every one that hangeth on a tree."

Horn—A horn symbolizes Gentile kings and the four world empires; Babylon, Media Persia, Greece and Rome. *(Read Daniel 2:19-43)* Horn is also symbolic of power and strength. *(Read Psalm 18:2)*

Zechariah 1:18 19- "Then lifted I up mine eyes, and saw, and behold four horns. And I said unto the angel that talked with me, What be these? And he answered me, These are the horns which have scattered Judah, Israel, and Jerusalem."

1st Samuel 2:10 "The adversaries of the LORD shall be broken to pieces; out of heaven shall he thunder upon them: the LORD shall judge the ends of the earth; and he shall give strength unto his king, and exalt the horn of his anointed."

Hyssop—A herb or a flower used for purification and cleansing from the defilement of sin. Washing with hyssop typified redemption by the Blood of Jesus. *(Read Hebrews 9:19-27)*

Psalm 51:7 "Purge me with hyssop, and I shall be clean: wash me, and I shall be whiter than snow."

Hebrews 9:28 "So Christ was once offered to bear the sins of many; and unto them that look for him shall he appear the second time without sin unto salvation."

Incense, Altar—The smoke and fragrance from the incense that ascended to God is a type of Christ who intercedes for us taking our prayers up to God. Prayer is accompanied by praise and sacrifices, which ascend to God pleasing Him as the believer functions as a priest.

Exodus 30:1 "And thou shalt make an altar to burn incense upon: of shittim wood shalt thou make it."

Hebrews 13:15-16 "By him therefore let us offer the sacrifice of praise to God continually, that is, the fruit of our lips giving thanks to his name. But to do good and to communicate forget not: for with such sacrifices God is well pleased."

Incense—It is also symbolic of worship. Strange incense is worship and praise that is forbidden because it is usually tainted with sensuality, formality, religiosity or praise to men and organizations that replace Christ. *(Read Leviticus 10:1)*

Exodus 30:9 "Ye shall offer no strange incense thereon, nor burnt sacrifice, nor meat offering; neither shall ye pour drink offering thereon."

Isaac—Obedient to the will of his father, even if it meant dying. Christ is a type of Isaac in that sense. He obeyed the will of God to die as a sacrifice for the sins of man.

Genesis 22:9 "And they came to the place which God had told him of; and Abraham built an altar there, and laid the wood in order, and bound Isaac his son, and laid him on the altar upon the wood."

Mark 14:35-36 "And he went forward a little, and fell on the ground, and prayed that, if it were possible, the hour might pass from him. And he said, Abba, Father, all things are possible unto thee; take away this cup from me: nevertheless not what I will, but what thou wilt."

Jacob—A type of Israel who strayed away, yet was kept and cared for and eventually restored by Jehovah because of His covenant with them.

Genesis 29:1 "Then Jacob went on his journey, and came into the land of the people of the east."

Romans 11:26-27 "And so all Israel shall be saved: as it is written, There shall come out of Zion the Deliverer, and shall turn away ungodliness from Jacob: For this is my covenant unto them, when I shall take away their sins."

Jordan—Passing over the Jordan River typifies the believer's passage from a life of sin and spiritual death into a new life that is spiritually rewarding.

Joshua 3:1 "And Joshua rose early in the morning; and they removed from Shittim, and came to Jordan, he and all the children of Israel, and lodged there before they passed over."

Ephesians 2:5-6 "Even when we were dead in sins, hath quickened us together with Christ, (by grace ye are saved;) And hath raised us up together, and made us sit together in heavenly places in Christ Jesus."

Joshua—His name means "Jehovah-Savior" and thus describes him as being a type of Christ, who is our defense and makes provisions for us. He is the "captain of our salvation."

Joshua 1:1-2 "Now after the death of Moses the servant of the LORD it came to pass, that the LORD spake unto Joshua the son of Nun, Moses' minister, saying, Moses my servant is dead; now therefore arise, go over this Jordan, thou, and all this people, unto the land which I do give to them, even to the children of Israel."

Hebrews 2:9-11 "But we see Jesus, who was made a little lower than the angels for the suffering of death, crowned with glory and honour; that he by the grace of God should taste death for every man. For it became him, for whom are all things, and by whom are all things, in bringing many sons unto glory, to make the captain of their salvation perfect through sufferings. For both he that sanctifieth and they who are sanctified are all of one: for which cause he is not ashamed to call them brethren."

Lamb—The lamb is the best offering to be used as a sacrifice for the remission of sin, and throughout the Bible is a type of Christ. It is consistent in its portrayal of the innocent dying for the guilty. Christ is the "Lamb of God" who took away the sins of the world. *(Read Hebrews 9:22)*

Genesis 4:4 "And Abel, he also brought of the firstlings of his flock and of the fat thereof. And the LORD had respect unto Abel and to his offering."

John 1:29 "The next day John seeth Jesus coming unto him, and saith, Behold the Lamb of God, which taketh away the sin of the world."

Laver—Prior to ministering before the altar, Jewish ministers were required to wash their hands and feet in a vessel called a "laver." This typifies the believer's need of cleansing before approaching the Lord; his heart should be clean. Also typified by the "laver" washing is baptism (the believer is cleansed from their sins).

Exodus 30:18 "Thou shalt also make a laver of brass, and his foot also of brass, to wash withal: and thou shalt put it between the tabernacle of the congregation and the altar, and thou shalt put water therein."

John 13:3-5 "Jesus knowing that the Father had given all things into his hands, and that he was come from God, and went to God; He riseth from supper, and laid aside his garments; and took a towel, and girded himself. After that he poureth water into a basin, and began to wash the disciples' feet, and to wipe them with the towel wherewith he was girded." *(Read John Chapter 13 and Ephesians 5:25-27)*

Leaven—Used in dough as a rising ingredient, leaven symbolizes evil moral influences that rise up in an individual believer or within a group of believers. False doctrine is also symbolic of leaven. *(Read Luke 12:1 and Mark 8:14-21)*

Genesis 19:3 "And he pressed upon them greatly; and they turned in unto him, and entered into his house; and he made them a feast, and did bake unleavened bread, and they did eat."

Matthew 13:33 "Another parable spake he unto them; The kingdom of heaven is like unto leaven, which a woman took, and hid in three measures of meal, till the whole was leavened."

Leprosy—This disease is symbolic of sin. It illustrates the unclean heart that will affect the value of the intended service for God. Leprosy required separation from the general population, and those having it sought prayer for healing from it and its stigma. Used by God in Numbers 12:9 as a punishment for her criticism of Moses, Miriam is plagued with the disease. *(Read Mark 1:40-42)*

Exodus 4:6 "And the LORD said furthermore unto him, Put now thine hand into thy bosom. And he put his hand into his bosom: and when he took it out, behold, his hand was leprous as snow."

Leviticus 13:2 "When a man shall have in the skin of his flesh a rising, a scab, or bright spot, and it be in the skin of his flesh like the plague of leprosy; then he shall be brought unto Aaron the priest, or unto one of his sons the priests."

Light—Christ is a type of light that shines in darkness. He is also the "Son of Righteousness," as seen in Malachi 4:2, who scatters darkness. Those who by faith are able to observe this spiritual light, become greater lights, which make reflection in darkness (or the world and its sinfulness). *(Read Matthew 22:34-40 and Luke 1:78-79)*

Genesis 1:16 "And God made two great lights; the greater light to rule the day, and the lesser light to rule the night: he made the stars also."

Philippians 2:15 "That ye may be blameless and harmless, the sons of God, without rebuke, in the midst of a crooked and perverse nation, among whom ye shine as lights in the world."

Linen—In Scripture, linen represents righteousness on a personal level. The height of the fine linen hanging in the Tabernacle typifies the righteousness of Christ that is above the standards of personal righteousness. *(Read Matthew 22:34-40)*

Exodus 27:9 "And thou shalt make the court of the tabernacle: for the south side southward there shall be hangings for the court of fine twined linen of an hundred cubits long for one side."

Romans 13:8-9 "Owe no man any thing, but to love one another: for he that loveth another hath fulfilled the law. For this, Thou shalt not commit adultery, Thou shalt not kill, Thou shalt not steal, Thou shalt not bear false witness, Thou shalt not covet; and if there be any other commandment, it is briefly comprehended in this saying, namely, Thou shalt love thy neighbour as thyself."

Manna—Small wafers that were sent from heaven by God to fulfill the desperate needs of His people, typifies Christ as the "Bread of Life." Coming into the world in a humble way, He satisfies the needs of those who believe in Him.

Exodus 16:35 "And the children of Israel did eat manna forty years, until they came to a land inhabited; they did eat manna, until they came unto the borders of the land of Canaan."

John 6:35 "And Jesus said unto them, I am the bread of life: he that cometh to me shall never hunger; and he that believeth on me shall never thirst."

Melchizedek—A king from Salem ("peace") and a priest of "the most High," received tithes from Abraham after which he blessed him. Melchizedek (whose name means "my king is righteous") typifies Christ, who is our King and High Priest forever. *(Read Hebrews 5:1-10 and Chapter 7).*

Genesis 14:18 "And Melchizedek king of Salem brought forth bread and wine: and he was the priest of the most high God."

Hebrews 6:20 "Whither the forerunner is for us entered, even Jesus, made an high priest for ever after the order of Melchizedek."

Moses—Sent by God to Egypt to deliver His people from bondage, Moses is a type of Christ who was sent by God to deliver mankind from sin. *(Read Exodus 3:1-6, Isaiah 61:1 and 1st Thessalonians 1:10)*

***Exodus* 3:7-12** "And the LORD said, I have surely seen the affliction of my people which are in Egypt, and have heard their cry by reason of their taskmasters; for I know their sorrows; And I am come down to deliver them out of the hand of the Egyptians, and to bring them up out of that land unto a good land and a large, unto a land flowing with milk and honey; unto the place of the Canaanites, and the Hittites, and the Amorites, and the Perizzites, and the Hivites, and the Jebusites. Now therefore, behold, the cry of the children of Israel is come unto me: and I have also seen the oppression wherewith the Egyptians oppress them. Come now therefore, and I will send thee unto Pharaoh, that thou mayest bring forth my people the children of Israel out of Egypt. And Moses said unto God, Who am I, that I should go unto Pharaoh, and that I should bring forth the children of Israel out of Egypt? And he said, Certainly I will be with thee; and this shall be a token unto thee, that I have sent thee: When thou hast brought forth the people out of Egypt, ye shall serve God upon this mountain."

***Luke* 4:18** "The Spirit of the Lord is upon me, because he hath anointed me to preach the gospel to the poor; he hath sent me to heal the brokenhearted, to preach deliverance to the captives, and recovering of sight to the blind, to set at liberty them that are bruised."

Mountains—A symbol of strength, stability and places where God and revelations could be found. Mountains were also places for solitude and prayer. In contrast to this, mountains are sometimes symbolic of difficulty, hindrances and obstacles that are encountered in life. They may also symbolize kingdoms and the Kingdom of God in Scripture. *(Read Genesis 22:14, Exodus 18:5, Jeremiah 51:25, Daniel 2:35 and Revelation 17:9)*

***Isaiah* 2:2** "And it shall come to pass in the last days, that the mountain of the LORD'S house shall be established in the top of the mountains, and shall be exalted above the hills; and all nations shall flow unto it."

Nazariteship—Symbolic of temporary separation for the purpose of consecration. *(Read Amos 2:11)*

***Numbers* 6:2** "Speak unto the children of Israel, and say unto them, When either man or woman shall separate themselves to vow a vow of a Nazarite, to separate themselves unto the LORD."

Ninevah—The capital of Assyria is symbolic of the world's pride, indulgence and vanity.

***Jonah* 1:2** "Arise, go to Nineveh, that great city, and cry against it; for their wickedness is come up before me."

Oak—Symbolizes strength.

Amos 2:9 "Yet destroyed I the Amorite before them, whose height was like the height of the cedars, and he was strong as the oaks; yet I destroyed his fruit from above, and his roots from beneath."

Ox—A type of Christ as a substitute offering. He is the strong yet patient servant of God who was able to endure the suffering of the cross. This sets an example for believers in their service for the Lord. *(Read 1st Corinthians 9:9-10 and Hebrews 12:1-2)*

Leviticus 1:3 "If his offering be a burnt sacrifice of the herd, let him offer a male without blemish: he shall offer it of his own voluntary will at the door of the tabernacle of the congregation before the LORD."

Philippians 2:5-8 "Let this mind be in you, which was also in Christ Jesus: Who, being in the form of God, thought it not robbery to be equal with God: But made himself of no reputation, and took upon him the form of a servant, and was made in the likeness of men: And being found in fashion as a man, he humbled himself, and became obedient unto death, even the death of the cross."

Perfume—Compounded especially by God, the perfume in the tabernacle was not meant to delight man but rather God. Perfume was symbolic of spiritual prayer and praise.

Exodus 30:34-38 "And the LORD said unto Moses, Take unto thee sweet spices, stacte, and onycha, and galbanum; these sweet spices with pure frankincense: of each shall there be a like weight: And thou shalt make it a perfume, a confection after the art of the apothecary, tempered together, pure and holy: And thou shalt beat some of it very small, and put of it before the testimony in the tabernacle of the congregation, where I will meet with thee: it shall be unto you most holy. And as for the perfume which thou shalt make, ye shall not make to yourselves according to the composition thereof: it shall be unto thee holy for the LORD. Whosoever shall make like unto that, to smell thereto, shall even be cut off from his people."

John 4:23-24 "But the hour cometh, and now is, when the true worshippers shall worship the Father in spirit and in truth: for the Father seeketh such to worship him. God is a Spirit: and they that worship him must worship him in spirit and in truth."

Potter—Symbolic of God who creates His vessels to perfection. Here it symbolizes Israel whom He'll have to break and re-create. *(Read Jeremiah 18:2-4)*

Jeremiah 18:2 "Arise, and go down to the potter's house, and there I will cause thee to hear my words."

Rainbow—A symbol of God's promise to Noah to never again destroy the earth by water. The rainbow sealed the covenant.

Genesis 9:13 "I do set my bow in the cloud, and it shall be for a token of a covenant between me and the earth."

Ram—A type of Christ who was a substitute offering.

Genesis 22:13 "And Abraham lifted up his eyes, and looked, and behold behind him a ram caught in a thicket by his horns: and Abraham went and took the ram, and offered him up for a burnt offering in the stead of his son."

Hebrews 10:8-10 "Above when he said, Sacrifice and offering and burnt offerings and offering for sin thou wouldest not, neither hadst pleasure therein; which are offered by the law; Then said he, Lo, I come to do thy will, O God. He taketh away the first, that he may establish the second. By the which will we are sanctified through the offering of the body of Jesus Christ once for all."

Red Heifer—Symbolic of cleansing and consecration of the believer from worldly defilement which can occur during his walk of faith. *(Read Hebrews Chapter 10)*

Numbers 19:2 "This is the ordinance of the law which the LORD hath commanded, saying, Speak unto the children of Israel, that they bring thee a red heifer without spot, wherein is no blemish, and upon which never came yoke."

Hebrews 9:12-14 "Neither by the blood of goats and calves, but by his own blood he entered in once into the holy place, having obtained eternal redemption for us. For if the blood of bulls and of goats, and the ashes of an heifer sprinkling the unclean, sanctifieth to the purifying of the flesh: How much more shall the blood of Christ, who through the eternal Spirit offered himself without spot to God, purge your conscience from dead works to serve the living God?"

Remnant—Typifies those who are left and remain faithful through great trial, testing and tribulation. *(Read Isaiah 19,Ezra 9:8, Romans 9:27 and Revelation 12:17)*

Daniel 3:17 "If it be so, our God whom we serve is able to deliver us from the burning fiery furnace, and he will deliver us out of thine hand, O king."

Romans 11:5 "Even so then at this present time also there is a remnant according to the election of grace."

Rock—The rock being struck and water coming from it typifies Christ dying, and the Holy Spirit's descent which confirmed redemption from sin. *(Read John 7:37-39)* The rock also represents a place of shelter, which typifies Christ as being a safe place or a strong foundation. *(Read Psalms 31:3)*

Exodus 17:6 "Behold, I will stand before thee there upon the rock in Horeb; and thou shalt smite the rock, and there shall come water out of it, that the people may drink. And Moses did so in the sight of the elders of Israel."

John 4:14 "But whosoever drinketh of the water that I shall give him shall never thirst; but the water that I shall give him shall be in him a well of water springing up into everlasting life."

Exodus 33:18-23 "And he said, I beseech thee, show me thy glory. And he said, I will make all my goodness pass before thee, and I will proclaim the name of the LORD before thee; and will be gracious to whom I will be gracious, and will show mercy on whom I will show mercy. And he said, Thou canst not see my face: for there shall no man see me, and live. And the LORD said, Behold, there is a place by me, and thou shalt stand upon a rock: And it shall come to pass, while my glory passeth by, that I will put thee in a cleft of the rock, and will cover thee with my hand while I pass by: And I will take away mine hand, and thou shalt see my back parts: but my face shall not be seen."

Matthew 7:24-25 "Therefore whosoever heareth these sayings of mine, and doeth them, I will liken him unto a wise man, which built his house upon a rock: And the rain descended, and the floods came, and the winds blew, and beat upon that house; and it fell not: for it was founded upon a rock."

Rod, Aaron's—The budding of Aaron's rod typifies the resurrection of Christ which proved Him to be above all other priests and rulers. His power and authority are divine and is therefore (unlike the others) not temporary but forever.

Numbers 17:8 "And it came to pass, that on the morrow Moses went into the tabernacle of witness; and, behold, the rod of Aaron for the house of Levi was budded, and brought forth buds, and bloomed blossoms, and yielded almonds."

Hebrews 7:23-28 "And they truly were many priests, because they were not suffered to continue by reason of death: But this man, because he continueth ever, hath an unchangeable priesthood. Wherefore he is able also to save them to the uttermost that come unto God by him, seeing he ever liveth to make intercession for them. For such an high priest became us, who is holy, harmless, undefiled, separate from sinners, and made higher than the heavens; Who needeth not daily, as those high priests, to offer up sacrifice, first for his own sins, and then for the people's: for this he did once, when he offered up himself. For the law maketh men high priests which have infirmity; but the word of the oath, which was since the law, maketh the Son, who is consecrated for evermore."

Rod—Symbol of:

Authority:

Jeremiah 48:17 "All ye that are about him, bemoan him; and all ye that know his name, say, How is the strong staff broken, and the beautiful rod!"

Correction "The Rod of Correction"

Proverbs 13:24 "He that spareth his rod hateth his son: but he that loveth him chasteneth him betimes."

Guidance "The Shepherd's Rod"

Psalm 23:4 "Yea, though I walk through the valley of the shadow of death, I will fear no evil: for thou art with me; thy rod and thy staff they comfort me."

Roll—This is a symbol of the Word of God that was written either by Him or man.

Zechariah 5:1 "Then I turned, and lifted up mine eyes, and looked, and behold a flying roll." *(Read Ezra 6:2, Jeremiah 36:2, Ezekiel 3:1-3)*

Salt—Symbolic of purification, preservation and endurance. Here it is added to the sacrifice to confirm its purity and endurance.

Leviticus 2:1 "And when any will offer a meat offering unto the LORD, his offering shall be of fine flour; and he shall pour oil upon it, and put frankincense thereon."

Sanctification—Symbolic of being set aside (holiness) for service by God.

Leviticus 21:8 "Thou shalt sanctify him therefore; for he offereth the bread of thy God: he shall be holy unto thee: for I the LORD, which sanctify you, am holy."

Sea—Symbolizes masses of people that are gathered together without organization. *(Read Matthew 13:47 and Revelation 13:1)*

Daniel 7:2 "Daniel spake and said, I saw in my vision by night, and, behold, the four winds of the heaven strove upon the great sea."

Serpent—Another name for Satan; serpents are symbolic of evil.

Revelation 12:9 "And the great dragon was cast out, that old serpent, called the Devil, and Satan, which deceiveth the whole world: he was cast out into the earth, and his angels were cast out with him."

Serpent, Brazen—A type of Christ being lifted on the cross bearing our sins so that we are delivered and can have eternal life. *(Read Numbers 21:4-9)*

Numbers 21:9 "And Moses made a serpent of brass, and put it upon a pole, and it came to pass, that if a serpent had bitten any man, when he beheld the serpent of brass, he lived."

John 3:14-16 "And as Moses lifted up the serpent in the wilderness, even so must the Son of man be lifted up: That whosoever believeth in him should not perish, but have eternal life. For God so loved the world, that he gave his only begotten Son, that whosoever believeth in him should not perish, but have everlasting life."

Tabernacle—Typifies the place where God abides among His people. It is also called a tent, sanctuary, booth or House of the Lord. The Tabernacle of the Old Testament was a shadow of the "true Tabernacle" which through Christ, became a reality. *(Read Leviticus 23:42; 1st Kings 6:1; Hebrews 8:1-4 and Hebrews Chapter 10)*

Exodus 25:9 "According to all that I show thee, after the pattern of the tabernacle, and the pattern of all the instruments thereof, even so shall ye make it."

Hebrews 8:5 "Who serve unto the example and shadow of heavenly things, as Moses was admonished of God when he was about to make the tabernacle: for, See, saith he, that thou make all things according to the pattern showed to thee in the mount."

Trumpets—Used symbolically to gather God's people.

Leviticus 23:24 "Speak unto the children of Israel, saying, In the seventh month, in the first day of the month, shall ye have a Sabbath, a memorial of blowing of trumpets, an holy convocation."

Veil of Tabernacle—Used to prevent direct access to God, the veil of the Tabernacle is a type of Christ's human body. When He died on the cross, the veil was torn by God symbolizing that divine justice (which was above the Law) had been met, allowing a new and better approach (though Christ) to God. This ended the dispensation of the Law. *(Read Matthew 26:26-29 and 27:51)*

Exodus 26:31 "And thou shalt make a veil of blue, and purple, and scarlet, and fine twined linen of cunning work: with cherubims shall it be made."

Hebrews 10:20 "By a new and living way, which he hath consecrated for us, through the veil, that is to say, his flesh."

Washing—A type of consecration from defilement. Under the Law of the Old Testament, washing is with water. Under Grace in the New Testament, washing is with the Word. Thus, the Word also convicts, washes the believer's heart and releases his mind from guilt (providing restoration).

The believer is then able (with a clear conscience) to continue his walk with the Lord and continue his service for Him.

***Numbers** 19:9* "And a man that is clean shall gather up the ashes of the heifer, and lay them up without the camp in a clean place, and it shall be kept for the congregation of the children of Israel for a water of separation: it is a purification for sin."

***Ephesians** 5:26* "That he might sanctify and cleanse it with the washing of water by the word"

Water—A symbol of:

Purification and Consecration

***Numbers** 31:23* "Every thing that may abide the fire, ye shall make it go through the fire, and it shall be clean: nevertheless it shall be purified with the water of separation: and all that abideth not the fire ye shall make go through the water."

New Life

***John** 7:37-39* "In the last day, that great day of the feast, Jesus stood and cried, saying, If any man thirst, let him come unto me, and drink. He that believeth on me, as the scripture hath said, out of his belly shall flow rivers of living water. (But this spake he of the Spirit, which they that believe on him should receive: for the Holy Ghost was not yet given; because that Jesus was not yet glorified.)"

Holy Spirit for Power

***Acts** 1:5-8* "For John truly baptized with water; but ye shall be baptized with the Holy Ghost not many days hence. When they therefore were come together, they asked of him, saying, Lord, wilt thou at this time restore again the kingdom to Israel? And he said unto them, It is not for you to know the times or the seasons, which the Father hath put in his own power. But ye shall receive power, after that the Holy Ghost is come upon you: and ye shall be witnesses unto me both in Jerusalem, and in all Judaea, and in Samaria, and unto the uttermost part of the earth." ❖

NOTES

NOTES

Chapter 3

Symbolism in Revelation

The Seven Seal Book

This is the "Book of Redemption."

***Revelation** 5:1-4* "And I saw in the right hand of him that sat on the throne a book written within and on the backside, sealed with seven seals. And I saw a strong angel proclaiming with a loud voice, Who is worthy to open the book, and to loose the seals thereof? And no man in heaven, nor in earth, neither under the earth, was able to open the book, neither to look thereon. And I wept much, because no man was found worthy to open and to read the book, neither to look thereon."

White Horse Rider

He is the symbol of the "Willful King" (the Antichrist) who employs his own will, making demands to be worshipped as God.

***Revelation** 6:1-2* "And I saw when the Lamb opened one of the seals, and I heard, as it were the noise of thunder, one of the four beasts saying, Come and see. And I saw, and behold a white horse: and he that sat on him had a bow; and a crown was given unto him: and he went forth conquering, and to conquer."

The Red Horse

A symbol of the great blood shed and destruction which was prophesied by Christ in Matthew 24:6-7. The Great Sword the rider carries is symbolic of war.

***Revelation** 6:3-4* "And when he had opened the second seal, I heard the second beast say, Come and see. And there went out another horse that was red: and power was given to him that sat thereon to take peace from the earth, and that they should kill one another: and there was given unto him a great sword."

The Black Horse

The Black Horse speaks of the famine and death that is to come because of war resulting in man's inability to farm. The scale represents the small portions of grain that will be rationed.

***Revelation** 6:5-6* "And when he had opened the third seal, I heard the third beast say, Come and see. And I beheld, and lo a black horse; and he that sat on him had a pair of balances in his hand. And I heard a voice in the midst of the four beasts say, A measure of wheat for a penny, and three measures of barley for a penny; and see thou hurt not the oil and the wine."

The Pale Horse

Following the famine is death and hell of which this horse is symbolic.

Revelation 6:7-8 "And when he had opened the fourth seal, I heard the voice of the fourth beast say, Come and see. And I looked, and behold a pale horse: and his name that sat on him was Death, and Hell followed with him. And power was given unto them over the fourth part of the earth, to kill with sword, and with hunger, and with death, and with the beasts of the earth.'

The Sun Clothed Woman, Man Child, The Dragon

The sun clothed woman is symbolic of Israel who will bring forth a "Man Child" who is Christ. The Dragon is symbolic of Satan whose intent is to destroy the child.

Revelation 12:1-6 "And there appeared a great wonder in heaven; a woman clothed with the sun, and the moon under her feet, and upon her head a crown of twelve stars: And she being with child cried, travailing in birth, and pained to be delivered. And there appeared another wonder in heaven; and behold a great red dragon, having seven heads and ten horns, and seven crowns upon his heads. And his tail drew the third part of the stars of heaven, and did cast them to the earth: and the dragon stood before the woman which was ready to be delivered, for to devour her child as soon as it was born. And she brought forth a man child, who was to rule all nations with a rod of iron: and her child was caught up unto God, and to his throne. And the woman fled into the wilderness, where she hath a place prepared of God, that they should feed her there a thousand two hundred and threescore days."

The Beast out of the Sea

The Beast out of the Sea pretends to be an advocate for the Jews and have great concern for mankind, but he has contradicting characteristics. He is deceitful and cunning in the execution of his fiery power and implementation of his policies. Being able to succeed, he blasphemes and positions himself for worship as a god.

Revelation 13:1-10 "And I stood upon the sand of the sea, and saw a beast rise up out of the sea, having seven heads and ten horns, and upon his horns ten crowns, and upon his heads the name of blasphemy. And the beast which I saw was like unto a leopard, and his feet were as the feet of a bear, and his mouth as the mouth of a lion: and the dragon gave him his power, and his seat, and great authority. And I saw one of his heads as it were wounded to death; and his deadly wound was healed: and all the world wondered after the beast. And they worshipped the dragon which gave power unto the beast: and they worshipped the beast, saying, Who is like unto the beast? who is able to make war with him? And there was given unto him a mouth speaking great things and blasphemies; and power was given unto him to continue forty and two months. And he opened his mouth in blasphemy against God, to blaspheme his name, and his tabernacle, and them that dwell in heaven. And it was given unto him to make war with the saints, and to overcome them: and power was given him over all kindreds, and tongues, and nations. And all that dwell upon the earth shall worship him, whose names are not written in the book of life of the Lamb slain from the foundation of the world. If any man have an ear, let him hear. He that leadeth into captivity shall go into captivity: he that killeth with the sword must be killed with the sword. Here is the patience and the faith of the saints."

The Beast out of the Earth

This is the Antichrist who will deceive many causing them to receive his mark, 666. His powers are representative of the world system which is influenced by Satan.

Revelation 13:11-18 "And I beheld another beast coming up out of the earth; and he had two horns like a lamb, and he spake as a dragon. And he exerciseth all the power of the first beast before him, and causeth the earth and them which dwell therein to worship the first beast, whose deadly wound was healed. And he doeth great wonders, so that he maketh fire come down from heaven on the earth in the sight of men, And deceiveth them that dwell on the earth by the means of those miracles which he had power to do in the sight of the beast; saying to them that dwell on the earth, that they should make an image to the beast, which had the wound by a sword, and did live. And he had power to give life unto the image of the beast, that the image of the beast should both speak, and cause that as many as would not worship the image of the beast should be killed. And he causeth all, both small and great, rich and poor, free and bond, to receive a mark in their right hand, or in their foreheads: And that no man might buy or sell, save he that had the mark, or the name of the beast, or the number of his name. Here is wisdom. Let him that hath understanding count the number of the beast: for it is the number of a man; and his number is Six hundred threescore and six."

The Lamb upon Mt. Zion

The Lamb is Christ and Mt. Zion is one of the places considered to be a place where God dwelled. The virgins are the 144,000 who prevailed the sin of fornication during the End Times. The new song does not speak of redemption provided by the Blood, but rather from the sin of fornication.

Revelation 14:1-5 "And I looked, and, lo, a Lamb stood on the Mount Zion, and with him a hundred forty and four thousand, having his Father's name written in their foreheads. And I heard a voice from heaven, as the voice of many waters, and as the voice of a great thunder: and I heard the voice of harpers harping with their harps: And they sung as it were a new song before the throne, and before the four beasts, and the elders: and no man could learn that song but the hundred and forty and four thousand, which were redeemed from the earth. These are they which were not defiled with women; for they are virgins. These are they which follow the Lamb whithersoever he goeth. These were redeemed from among men, being the firstfruits unto God and to the Lamb. And in their mouth was found no guile: for they are without fault before the throne of God."

The Crowned Reaper with a Sickle

The reaper is Christ who will harvest the Gentile nations. The harvest and vintage is judicial and points to the gathering of nations and the War of Armageddon. The illustration of harvest, sickle and winepress symbolizes the Lord plunging His judgement in the midst of the battle resulting in great bloodshed. *(Read Chapter 16: 13-16 and Chapter 19)*

Revelation 14:14-20 "And I looked, and behold a white cloud, and upon the cloud one sat like unto the Son of man, having on his head a golden crown, and in his hand a sharp sickle. And another angel came out of the temple, crying with a loud voice to him that sat on the cloud, Thrust in thy sickle, and reap: for the time is come for thee to reap; for the harvest of the earth is ripe. And he that sat on the cloud thrust in his sickle on the earth; and the earth was reaped. And another angel came out of the temple which is in heaven, he also having a sharp sickle. And another angel came out from the altar, which had power over fire; and cried with a loud cry to him that had the sharp sickle, saying, Thrust in thy sharp sickle, and gather the clusters of the vine of the earth; for her grapes are fully ripe. And the angel thrust in his sickle into the earth, and gathered the vine of the earth, and cast it into the great winepress of the wrath of God. And the winepress was trodden without the city, and blood came out of the winepress, even unto the horse bridles, by the space of a thousand and six hundred furlongs."

The Seven Vial Judgements

The seven vial judgements speak of bowls of God's wrath that will be poured upon the earth. *(Read Revelation Chapters 15 and 16)*

The Great Whore

"The great whore" is symbolic of ecclesiastical Babylon, the church that is in a state of apostasy. The political Babylon, symbolic of the world system, eventually destroys it.

Revelation 17:1 "And there came one of the seven angels which had the seven vials, and talked with me, saying unto me, Come hither; I will show unto thee the judgment of the great whore that sitteth upon many waters.'

The Lamb's Wife

"The Lamb's wife" is symbolic of the church that is made up of saints who are righteous. The Lamb is Christ.

Revelation 19:7-8 "Let us be glad and rejoice, and give honour to him: for the marriage of the Lamb is come, and his wife hath made herself ready. And to her was granted that she should be arrayed in fine linen, clean and white: for the fine linen is the righteousness of saints." ❖

NOTES

NOTES

CHAPTER 4

THE TABERNACLE

TABERNACLE OFFERINGS

BURNT OFFERING (SWEET SAVOR OFFERINGS)

Voluntary is the key word describing this offering. It is given freely to atone for sin, making it the best offering. This offering typifies Christ who was blameless yet offered Himself voluntarily to atone for man's sins. Christ is a type of "substitute" on behalf of the sinner . . . a sweet savor offering. *(Read Hebrews 10:5-7)*

Leviticus 1:3 "If his offering be a burnt sacrifice of the herd, let him offer a male without blemish: he shall offer it of his own voluntary will at the door of the tabernacle of the congregation before the LORD."

Hebrews 10:9-10 "Then said he, Lo, I come to do thy will, O God. He taketh away the first, that he may establish the second. By which will we are sanctified through the offering of the body of Jesus Christ once for all."

MEAL OFFERING (SWEET SAVOR OFFERING)

Omitting leaven (sin) and honey (natural sweetness), only the best ingredients were used in this offering (also called the Meat Offering). The fine flour is symbolic of the blameless life and pure character of Christ. Oil is a symbol of the Holy Spirit along with frankincense (perfection). Also symbolized in this offering is the suffering of Christ. *(Read Matthew 27:27-31 and Hebrews 2:18)*

Leviticus 2:1-2 "And when any will offer a meat offering unto the LORD, his offering shall be of fine flour; and he shall pour oil upon it, and put frankincense thereon: And he shall bring it to Aaron's sons the priests: and he shall take thereout his handful of the flour thereof, and of the oil thereof, with all the frankincense thereof; and the priest shall burn the memorial of it upon the altar, to be an offering made by fire, of a sweet savour unto the LORD."

SIN OFFERING (NON-SWEET SAVOR OFFERING)

Here Christ is typified as the substitute offering that bears the sinner's sin and his disobedience. *(Read Isaiah 53 and Psalms 22)*

Leviticus 4:3 "If the priest that is anointed do sin according to the sin of the people; then let him bring for his sin, which he hath sinned, a young bullock without blemish unto the LORD for a sin offering."

1st Peter 2:24 "Who his own self bare our sins in his own body on the tree, that we, being dead to sins, should live unto righteousness: by whose stripes ye were healed."

TRESPASS OFFERING (NON-SWEET SAVOR OFFERING)

This offering was made to make amends or restitution for sins that were unintentional or caused harm and injury to another. Christ is seen in the Trespass Offering as making atonement for the harm caused by the sin.

Leviticus 5:6 "And he shall bring his trespass offering unto the LORD for his sin which he hath sinned, a female from the flock, a lamb or a kid of the goats, for a sin offering; and the priest shall make an atonement for him concerning his sin."

PEACE OFFERING (SWEET SAVOR OFFERING)

Christ was the offering that made peace between the believer and God, and His sacrifice made fellowship possible with God. Christ is, therefore, a type of peace offering. The peace offering speaks of peace between the offender, the priest and God. The best part of the offering was given to the priest for food. The offender then showed that he accepted the work of the priest who went before God on his behalf. So God, who provided this order, is satisfied and reconciles the sinner. In essence, all are in fellowship with each other. *(Read Leviticus 7:11-12; 31-34)*

Leviticus 3:1 "And if his oblation be a sacrifice of peace offering, if he offer it of the herd; whether it be a male or female, he shall offer it without blemish before the LORD."

Colossians 1:20 "And, having made peace through the blood of his cross, by him to reconcile all things unto himself; by him, I say, whether they be things in earth, or things in heaven."

THE LAW OF THE OFFERINGS (Leviticus 6:8-30 and 7:1-21)

The order of these offerings is helpful in giving us a clearer understanding of the atonement process. The Burnt Offering is a type of Christ who died for our sins. The Meal Offering symbolizes His perfection. The Sin Offering made atonement for the guilt of sin, while the Trespass Offering atoned for its injury. All are followed by the Peace Offering, which represents the fellowship that follows between the offender and God.

Savor is descriptive of the pleasure God took in the significance or meaning of the offerings. The Burnt Offering, Meal Offering (or Meat Offering) and the Peace Offering were "Sweet Savor Offerings" which pleased God because it spoke of vindication and restoration. The Sin Offering and Trespass Offering were "Non-Sweet Savor Offerings" which displeased God because they represented the offense.

In all, the offerings prove the love of God and the richness of His mercy.

Ephesians 2:4-7 "But God, who is rich in mercy, for his great love wherewith he loved us, Even when we were dead in sins, hath quickened us together with Christ, (by grace ye are saved;) And hath raised us up together, and made us sit together in heavenly places in Christ Jesus: That in the ages to come he might show the exceeding riches of his grace in his kindness toward us through Christ Jesus."

TABERNACLE COLORS, MATERIALS AND ELEMENTS

Colors and materials are used in the Old Testament as figurative similarities to other things bringing spiritual consistency and harmony.

Exodus 25:3-4 "And this is the offering which ye shall take of them; gold, and silver, and brass. And blue, and purple, and scarlet, and fine linen, and goats' hair."

Blue—Heavenly

Brass—Judgement (also copper or bronze)

Gold—Divine Glory, Kingship

Purple—Royalty, Worn mostly by royalty due to the expense in making the dye

Silver—Redemption, having gone through purification or refinement

Scarlet—Sacrifice, This color is mostly crimson representing safety

Fine Linen—Righteousness of the Lamb of God or Christ

Frankincense—Perfection of Christ

Perfume—Prayer and Praise

Oil—Sacred Anointing symbolizing consecration of the priests (poured on the meal offering, it is symbolic of the Holy Spirit's presence and power which was evident in the life of Christ who is symbolized by the offering)

Salt—Representing purification and preservation from sin *Fire*—

Symbolic of God's judgement, purification and His presence

Water—Judgement and ceremonial cleansing

Animals Acceptable for Sacrifice

Bullock

Substitute for the Burnt Offering typifies Christ as the servant of God who was obedient unto death. *(See Ox)*

***Isaiah* 52:13-15** "Behold, my servant shall deal prudently, he shall be exalted and extolled, and be very high. As many were astonied at thee; his visage was so marred more than any man, and his form more than the sons of men: So shall he sprinkle many nations; the kings shall shut their mouths at him: for that which had not been told them shall they see; and that which they had not heard shall they consider."

***Hebrews* 12:1-2** "Wherefore seeing we also are compassed about with so great a cloud of witnesses, let us lay aside every weight, and the sin which doth so easily beset us, and let us run with patience the race that is set before us, Looking unto Jesus the author and finisher of our faith; who for the joy that was set before him endured the cross, despising the shame, and is set down at the right hand of the throne of God."

Goat

Used for Burnt and Sin Offerings, it is type of Christ who is a substitute.

***Leviticus* 4:24** "And he shall lay his hand upon the head of the goat, and kill it in the place where they kill the burnt offering before the LORD: it is a sin offering."

Lamb

Deliverance and redemption is through Christ, typified as the "Lamb of God" who took away the sins of the world. *(Read Exodus 12:6, Luke 9:31, 1st Corinthians 5:7 and Hebrews 9:22)*

***Leviticus* 1:10** "And if his offering be of the flocks, namely, of the sheep, or of the goats, for a burnt sacrifice; he shall bring it a male without blemish."

***Hebrews* 9:12-14** "Neither by the blood of goats and calves, but by his own blood he entered in once into the holy place, having obtained eternal redemption for us. For if the blood of bulls and of goats, and the ashes of an heifer sprinkling the unclean, sanctifieth to the purifying of the flesh: How much more shall the blood of Christ, who through the eternal Spirit offered himself without spot to God, purge your conscience from dead works to serve the living God?"

Turtledove (Pigeon)

These birds are symbolic of grief or mourning and were offered by the poor. This typifies Christ who became poor and died for our sins so we may benefit, because through Him we are made rich. *(Read Philippians 2:5-8)*

***Leviticus** 5:7* "And if he be not able to bring a lamb, then he shall bring for his trespass, which he hath committed, two turtledoves, or two young pigeons, unto the LORD; one for a sin offering, and the other for a burnt offering."

*2nd **Corinthians** 8:9* "For ye know the grace of our Lord Jesus Christ, that, though he was rich, yet for your sakes he became poor, that ye through his poverty might be rich." ❖

NOTES

NOTES

Chapter 5

Types of Christ

Aaron	Exodus 28:1	→	Hebrews 5
Abel	Genesis 4:2	→	Hebrews 9:22
Adam	Genesis 5:1	→	John 3:6
Altar (of Incense)	Exodus 30:1	→	Hebrews 7:25
Ark (Noah's)	Genesis 6:14	→	Hebrews 11:7
Benjamin	Genesis 35:18	→	Luke 11:7
Candlestick (golden)	Exodus 25:31	→	John 8:12
Coats of skin	Genesis 3:21	→	Revelation 19:8
David	1st Chronicles 17:7	→	Acts 15:16
Door (Gate)	Exodus 27:16	→	John 10:7
Goat	Leviticus 1:3	→	Galatians 3:13
Isaac	Genesis 22:9	→	Mark 14:35-36
Joshua	Joshua 1:1-2	→	Hebrews 2:9-11
Lamb	Leviticus 1:3	→	Hebrews 9:12-14
Light	Genesis 1:16	→	Philippians 2:15-16

Manna	Exodus 16:35	→	John 6:35
Melchizedek	Genesis 14:18	→	Hebrews 6:20
Moses	Exodus 3:7:12	→	Luke 4:18
Ox	Leviticus 1:3	→	Philippians 2:5-8
Passover	Exodus 12:11	→	1st Corinthians 5:7
Peace Offering	Leviticus 3:1	→	Colossians 1:20
Priesthood of Aaron	Exodus 28:1	→	Hebrews 5:1-4
Ram	Genesis 22:13	→	Hebrews 10:4-10
Rock	Exodus 17:6	→	John 4:14
Rod (Aaron's)	Number 17:8	→	Hebrews 7:23-28
Serpent (Brazen)	Numbers 21:9	→	John 3:14-16
Sin Offering	Leviticus 4:3	→	1st Peter 2:24
Trespass Offering	Leviticus 5:6	→	Hebrews 10:4-10
Turtledove	Leviticus 1:3	→	2nd Corinthians 8:9
Veil of the Tabernacle	Exodus 26:31	→	Hebrews 10:20

Notes

NOTES

Chapter 6

Numerology

Biblical numerology is the exploration of numbers that have symbolic meanings in Scripture. The study of numbers is heavily used in fetish, idolatrous, and strange and bizarre forms of worship. Numbers are used out of their Biblical context by many cults and the occult. Because of this, adherence to Biblical principals for the use of numbers found in Scripture is extremely important for proper interpretation. The following seven Basic Biblical Principles will serve as a safeguard against the dangers associated with Numerology.

Basic Biblical Principals

1) There are two ways to interpret numbers found in the Bible: Specific and Implied.
2) Certain numbers have specific meanings and are found in more than one place in the Bible.
3) The use and interpretation of specific numbers are found within the passage of Scripture in which they are being used.
4) Specified numbers are more noticeable than implied numbers and are therefore easier to understand.
5) Numbers may require addition or multiplication to gain an interpretation of their use in a passage of Scripture.
6) Implied numbers require more scrutiny of the passage of Scripture for an interpretation than specific numbers.
7) Always compare and cross-reference Scriptures so that interpretations of numbers are accurate. Remember that God's Word is consistent.

Symbolic Numbers

One

The number one is symbolic of unity and is the number of God *(Read Genesis 1:1, Genesis 2:21-24 and John 17:21-23)*

John 17:21-23 "That they all may be one; as thou, Father, art in me, and I in thee, that they also may be one in us: that the world may believe that thou hast sent me. And the glory which thou gavest me I have given them; that they may be one, even as we are one: I in them, and thou in me, that they may be made perfect in one; and that the world may know that thou hast sent me, and hast loved them, as thou hast loved me."

Two

The number two represents testimony and witness. In Scripture, bearing-witness to something necessitates using more than one person; usually two or more *(Read John 8:17, Matthew 18:16 and Revelation 11:3).* Two also speaks of separation of God's people from something or other people. We see this during the contest between God and Pharaoh in Exodus 8:22-23 and in Matthew 24:40, from two only one will be raptured to be with the Lord.

John 8:17 "It is also written in your law, that the testimony of two men is true."

Three

This is the number of the Godhead or Trinity which consists of God the Father, God the Son and God the Holy Spirit. The three separate and distinctive personalities of God, although plural, are united making Him one God (Matthew 28:19). When considering that one represents the number of God and unity, believers are therefore one with God, signifying divine completeness as seen in John 14:21. The believer is loved by Christ, The Father and receives the manifestation of the relationship through the Holy Spirit. *(Read John Chapters 14 and 15)*

Matthew 28:19 "Go ye therefore, and teach all nations, baptizing them in the name of the Father, and of the Son, and of the Holy Ghost."

Four

The earth, creation and the power of God is symbolized by the number four. *(Read Jeremiah 49:36 and Ezekiel 37:9)*

Revelation 7:1-3 "And after these things I saw four angels standing on the four corners of the earth, holding the four winds of the earth, that the wind should not blow on the earth, nor on the sea, nor on any tree. And I saw another angel ascending from the east, having the seal of the living God: and he cried with a loud voice to the four angels, to whom it was given to hurt the earth and the sea, Saying, Hurt not the earth, neither the sea, nor the trees, till we have sealed the servants of our God in their foreheads."

Seven

After creating the heavens and the earth and everything pertaining to them (declaring that each phase of it was to His perfection) God took His rest (Genesis 2:1-3). Seven is symbolic of perfection and/or completion. In the Book of Revelation the number seven is used frequently; perhaps because it is the book that speaks of the consummation of all things.

The Seven Churches—Revelation 1:4-8

The Seven Seals—Revelation Chapters 4-8:1

The Seven Trumpets—Revelation 8:2 through 11:19

The Seven Personages—Revelation 12:1 through 14:29

The Seven Bowl Judgments—Revelation 15:1 through 16:21

The Seven Dooms—Revelation 17:1 through 20:15

The Seven New Things—Revelation 21:1 through 22:21

Genesis 2:1-3 "Thus the heavens and the earth were finished, and all the host of them. And on the seventh day God ended his work which he had made; and he rested on the seventh day from all his work which he had made. And God blessed the seventh day, and sanctified it: because that in it he had rested from all his work which God created and made."

Eight

Eight implies starting over or new beginnings. In Genesis 17:12 a newborn male child is circumcised on the eighth day of life as a token of the covenant between God and man. The circumcision is symbolic of shedding away that which is unclean, a necessary requirement in order to receive covenant blessings. *(Read Leviticus 14:8-11)* The number eight also symbolizes the Resurrection of Christ. In Him, old things have passed away and everything begins anew. In John 20:26, it is the eighth day that the resurrected Christ appeared to His disciples. The work of Christ through His resurrection, ascension and priestly office in heaven is significant of the New Covenant. *(Read 1st John 3:18-22, 2nd Corinthians 5:17 and Hebrews 10:20)*

Genesis 17:12 "And he that is eight days old shall be circumcised among you, every man child in your generations, he that is born in the house, or bought with money of any stranger, which is not of thy seed."

Nine

The nine gifts of the Holy Spirit (1st Corinthians 12:1-20) and the nine fruit of the Spirit (Galatians 5:22-23) are the ways the Holy Spirit adds increase to our spiritual lives. Notice should be given to the time in which Christ died on the cross after declaring that His work of atonement was finished; it was the ninth hour. Here nine represents finality.

Matthew 27:46-50 "And about the ninth hour Jesus cried with a loud voice, saying, Eli, Eli, lama sabachthani? that is to say, My God, my God, why hast thou forsaken me? Some of them that stood there, when they heard that, said, This man calleth for Elias. And straightway one of them ran, and took a sponge, and filled it with vinegar, and put it on a reed, and gave him to drink. The rest said, Let be, let us see whether Elias will come to save him. Jesus, when he had cried again with a loud voice, yielded up the ghost."

Ten

Ten is symbolic of God's divine laws. In Exodus 34:28 He gave Moses the tenor of the covenant He made with him and Israel . . . The Ten Commandments. The law of giving tithe amounts to a tenth (Leviticus 27:30-33 and Numbers 18:21-32). The number ten is also used in the parables of Christ that teach the urgency of responsibility (Matthew 25:1-13).

Exodus 34:28 "And he was there with the LORD forty days and forty nights; he did neither eat bread, nor drink water. And he wrote upon the tables the words of the covenant, the ten commandments."

Twelve

The number that constitutes divine governmental order.

The Twelve Tribes of Israel

Genesis 49:28 "All these are the twelve tribes of Israel: and this is it that their father spake unto them, and blessed them; every one according to his blessing he blessed them."

The Twelve Apostles

Acts 1:13 "And when they were come in, they went up into an upper room, where abode both Peter, and James, and John, and Andrew, Philip, and Thomas, Bartholomew, and Matthew, James the son of Alphaeus, and Simon Zelotes, and Judas the brother of James."

Twenty-four

This number is symbolic of heavenly governmental order.

Revelation 4:4 "And round about the throne were four and twenty seats: and upon the seats I saw four and twenty elders sitting, clothed in white raiment; and they had on their heads crowns of gold."

Forty

Forty represents God's time-frame for testing. *(Read Acts 7:30)*

Numbers 14:33 "And your children shall wander in the wilderness forty years, and bear your whoredoms, until your carcases be wasted in the wilderness."

Matthew 4:1-2 "Then was Jesus led up of the Spirit into the wilderness to be tempted of the devil. And when he had fasted forty days and forty nights, he was afterward an hungered."

Fifty

Fifty represents the year of liberty and jubilee.

Leviticus 25:10 "And ye shall hallow the fiftieth year, and proclaim liberty throughout all the land unto all the inhabitants thereof: it shall be a jubilee unto you; and ye shall return every man unto his possession, and ye shall return every man unto his family."

Six-Six-Six

The mark of the Beast *(Read Revelation 11-17)*

Revelation 13:18 "Here is wisdom. Let him that hath understanding count the number of the beast: for it is the number of a man; and his number is Six hundred threescore and six." ❖

Notes

NOTES

Chapter 7

Other Types and Symbols

Symbols of the Holy Spirit

Dove

John 1:32 "And John bare record, saying, I saw the Spirit descending from heaven like a dove, and it abode upon him."

Water

John 7:38-39 "He that believeth on me, as the scripture hath said, out of his belly shall flow rivers of living water. (But this spake he of the Spirit, which they that believe on him should receive: for the Holy Ghost was not yet given; because that Jesus was not yet glorified.)"

Oil

Hebrews 1:9 "Thou has loved righteousness, and hated iniquity; therefore God, even thy God, hath anointed thee with the oil of gladness above thy fellows."

Seal

Ephesians 1:13 "In whom ye also trusted, after that ye heard the word of truth, the gospel of your salvation: in whom also after that ye believed, ye were sealed with that Holy Spirit of promise." *(Read Ephesians 4:30)*

Fire

Acts 2:3 "And there appeared unto them cloven tongues like as of fire, and it sat upon each of them."

The Church Typified by Brides

Eve

Just as Eve was dearly loved by Adam, the church (The Bride of Christ) is dearly loved by Christ.

Genesis 2:23 "And Adam said, This is now bone of my bones, and flesh of my flesh: she shall be called Woman, because she was taken out of Man."

Ephesians 5:25-27 "Husbands, love your wives, even as Christ also loved the church, and gave himself for it."

Rebecca

Rebecca is a type of church (ecclessia, meaning "called out") who is the Bride of Christ. The servant is a type of Holy Spirit that went out to get Rebecca for Isaac (who is a type of Christ, a bridegroom). After finding her, he gave testimony of her virtue. *(Read Genesis Chapter 24, John 16:13-14 and 1st Peter 1:8)*

Genesis 24:58-60 "And they called Rebekah, and said unto her, Wilt thou go with this man? And she said, I will go. And they sent away Rebekah their sister, and her nurse, and Abraham's servant, and his men. And they blessed Rebekah, and said unto her, Thou art our sister, be thou the mother of thousands of millions, and let thy seed possess the gate of those which hate them."

2nd Corinthians 11:2 "For I am jealous over you with godly jealousy: for I have espoused you to one husband, that I may present you as a chaste virgin to Christ."

Asenath

A type of gentile bride who is espoused to Christ. She is the gentile bride that was given to Joseph (who typifies Christ) during the time he was rejected by his brethren. *(Read Genesis Chapter 37)*

Genesis 41:43-45 "And he made him to ride in the second chariot which he had; and they cried before him, Bow the knee: and he made him ruler over all the land of Egypt. And Pharaoh said unto Joseph, I am Pharaoh, and without thee shall no man lift up his hand or foot in all the land of Egypt. And Pharaoh called Joseph's name Zaphnathpaaneah; and he gave him to wife Asenath the daughter of Potipherah priest of On. And Joseph went out over all the land of Egypt."

Acts 15:14 "Simeon hath declared how God at the first did visit the Gentiles, to take out of them a people for his name."

ZIPPORAH

A gentile bride that was given to Moses after he fled Egypt for killing an Egyptian and later rejected by his Hebrew brethren. Zipporah is a type of Church that was founded by Paul after the Jews rejected his testimony of Christ. *(Read Exodus Chapter 2:11-20 and Acts Chapter 18)*

Exodus 2:21 "And Moses was content to dwell with the man: and he gave Moses Zipporah his daughter."

Acts 18:6-8 "And when they opposed themselves, and blasphemed, he shook his raiment, and said unto them, Your blood be upon your own heads; I am clean: from henceforth I will go unto the Gentiles. And he departed thence, and entered into a certain man's house, named Justus, one that worshipped God, whose house joined hard to the synagogue. And Crispus, the chief ruler of the synagogue, believed on the Lord with all his house; and many of the Corinthians hearing believed, and were baptized."

Types of Dwelling Places of God

In the Old Testament

Tents

Genesis 9:27 "God shall enlarge Japheth, and he shall dwell in the tents of Shem; and Canaan shall be his servant."

The Tabernacle

1st Chronicles 17:2-6 "Then Nathan said unto David, Do all that is in thine heart; for God is with thee. And it came to pass the same night, that the word of God came to Nathan, saying, Go and tell David my servant, Thus saith the LORD, Thou shalt not build me an house to dwell in: For I have not dwelt in an house since the day that I brought up Israel unto this day; but have gone from tent to tent, and from one tabernacle to another. Wheresoever I have walked with all Israel, spake I a word to any of the judges of Israel, whom I commanded to feed my people, saying, Why have ye not built me an house of cedars?" *(Read Hebrews Chapter 9)*

The Temple

2nd Chronicles 6:1-2 "Then said Solomon, The LORD hath said that he would dwell in the thick darkness. But I have built an house of habitation for thee, and a place for thy dwelling for ever."

2nd Chronicles 7:1-2 "Now when Solomon had made an end of praying, the fire came down from heaven, and consumed the burnt offering and the sacrifices; and the glory of the LORD filled the house. And the priests could not enter into the house of the LORD, because the glory of the LORD had filled the LORD'S house."

In the New Testament

Christ

John 2:19 "Jesus answered and said unto them, Destroy this temple, and in three days I will raise it up."

Colossians 2:8-9 "Beware lest any man spoil you through philosophy and vain deceit, after the tradition of men, after the rudiments of the world, and not after Christ. For in him dwelleth all the fullness of the Godhead bodily." *(Read Matthew 26:61 and 27:40)*

The Church

1st Timothy 3:15 "But if I tarry long, that thou mayest know how thou oughtest to behave thyself in the house of God, which is the church of the living God, the pillar and ground of the truth."

Ephesians 2:20-22 "And are built upon the foundation of the apostles and prophets, Jesus Christ himself being the chief corner stone; In whom all the building fitly framed together groweth unto an holy temple in the Lord: In whom ye also are builded together for an habitation of God through the Spirit."

The Believer

1st John 4:11-15 "Beloved, if God so loved us, we ought also to love one another. No man hath seen God at any time. If we love one another, God dwelleth in us, and his love is perfected in us. Hereby know we that we dwell in him, and he in us, because he hath given us of his Spirit. And we have seen and do testify that the Father sent the Son to be the Saviour of the world. Whosoever shall confess that Jesus is the Son of God, God dwelleth in him, and he in God."

Future Place

Revelation 21: 1-6 "And I saw a new heaven and a new earth: for the first heaven and the first earth were passed away; and there was no more sea. And I John saw the holy city, new Jerusalem, coming down from God out of heaven, prepared as a bride adorned for her husband. And I heard a great voice out of heaven saying, Behold, the tabernacle of God is with men, and he will dwell with them, and they shall be his people, and God himself shall be with them, and be their God. And God shall wipe away all tears from their eyes; and there shall be no more death, neither sorrow, nor crying, neither shall there be any more pain: for the former things are passed away. And he that sat upon the throne said, Behold, I make all things new. And he said unto me, Write: for these words are true and faithful. And he said unto me, It is done. I am Alpha and Omega, the beginning and the end. I will give unto him that is athirst of the fountain of the water of life freely." ❖

NOTES

NOTES

In this series:

Volume 1: Introduction to Bible Doctrine
A Systematic Study of Seven Doctrines of the Christian Faith—Made Easy

Volume 2: Introduction to Bible Origin
A Study of the Formation of the Bible

Volume 3: Introduction to Typology and Symbolism
An Expository Study of Types and Symbols Found in the Bible

To order Bulk Volumes for Bible Study Groups go to:
www.swalkerpublications.com

To receive credit toward a Certificate in Biblical Studies for this series, send your request to: itmt@theinstituteoftheology.org

Attend Bible College at HOME!
The Institute of Theology and Ministry Training go to:
www.theinstituteoftheology.org

Made in the USA
Monee, IL
29 August 2021

76812106R00046